# · T R A V E L ·
# · D I A R Y ·

**SIMON & SCHUSTER**

AUSTRALIA

**TRAVEL DIARY**

First published in Australia in 1991 by
Simon & Schuster (Australia) Pty Limited
Suite 2, Lower Ground Floor,
14 -16 Suakin Street, Pymble NSW 2073
A CBS Company
Sydney  New York  London

Visit our website at www.simonsaysaustralia.com

Reprinted 1992,  1993
First revised and updated edition published in 1993
Reprinted 1994 (twice),  1995 (four times),  1996 (twice),
1998, 1999, 2001, 2002
Revised and reprinted in 2003
Reprinted 2005, 2006
© Simon & Schuster Australia 1991

ISBN 0 7318 0038 9

Designed and typset by Helen Semmler
Maps by Margaret Hastie, Ikon Computer Graphics
Set in ITC New Baskerville
Printed in Hong Kong through Phoenix Offset

# ▪ C O N T E N T S ▪

# ■ P E R S O N A L   D A T A ■

Name _____

Address _____

_____

Overseas contacts _____

_____

_____

_____

In case of emergency, please contact _____

_____

_____

_____

Blood group _____

Special medical information _____

_____

Religion _____

Passport number _____

Air ticket numbers _____

_____

_____

Credit card numbers _____

_____

_____

_____

# ▪ T R A V E L L E R ' S ▪
# ▪ S U R V I V A L   K I T ▪

Alarm clock/watch
Calculator (for calculating
  exchange rates)
Camera (with batteries and film)
Credit cards
Driver's licence
Earplugs
Electrical adaptor
Electrical adaptor for different
  plug types
Inflatable coathangers
Insect repellent
Maps
Mosquito net
Padlock
Passport
Pen
Plastic flask

Playing cards
Plug
Pocket clothes line
Safety pins (can clip pockets
  closed to prevent pickpocketing)
Sewing kit
Sunglasses
Swimming costumes
Swiss army knife
Toilet paper
Torch
Travel diary!
Traveller's cheques
Traveller's insurance policies
  (including medical insurance)
Vaccination certificates
Visas/ tourist cards
Water sterilising tablets

# ▪ F I R S T - A I D   K I T ▪

Antacid
Antibiotics (broad spectrum)
Anti-fungal cream (for athlete's
  foot and thrush)
Antihistamines (for prickly heat
  and other rashes)
Anti-malaria drugs (if applicable)
Antiseptic
Aspirin/paracetamol
Bandages
Bandaids
Calamine lotion

Chap stick for lips
Decongestant
Diarrhoea medicine
Eyedrops
Laxatives
Motion-sickness tablets
Prescription medicine
Spare pair of glasses/contact
  lenses
Sunscreen
Tampons (these are hard to get
  in some countries)

# ■ I T I N E R A R Y ■

Depart _____ Arrive _____

Accommodation _____

_____

Depart _____ Arrive _____

Accommodation _____

_____

Depart _____ Arrive _____

Accommodation _____

_____

Depart _____ Arrive _____

Accommodation _____

_____

Depart _____ Arrive _____

Accommodation _____

_____

Depart _____ Arrive _____

Accommodation _____

_____

Depart _____ Arrive _____

Accommodation _____

_____

_____

_____

# ■ I T I N E R A R Y ■

Depart ———————————— Arrive ————————————
Accommodation ——————————————————————————————
————————————————————————————————————————————————

Depart ———————————— Arrive ————————————
Accommodation ——————————————————————————————
————————————————————————————————————————————————

Depart ———————————— Arrive ————————————
Accommodation ——————————————————————————————
————————————————————————————————————————————————

Depart ———————————— Arrive ————————————
Accommodation ——————————————————————————————
————————————————————————————————————————————————

Depart ———————————— Arrive ————————————
Accommodation ——————————————————————————————
————————————————————————————————————————————————

Depart ———————————— Arrive ————————————
Accommodation ——————————————————————————————
————————————————————————————————————————————————

Depart ———————————— Arrive ————————————
Accommodation ——————————————————————————————
————————————————————————————————————————————————
————————————————————————————————————————————————
————————————————————————————————————————————————

# ■ I T I N E R A R Y ■

Depart _____ Arrive _____

Accommodation _____

_____

Depart _____ Arrive _____

Accommodation _____

_____

Depart _____ Arrive _____

Accommodation _____

_____

Depart _____ Arrive _____

Accommodation _____

_____

Depart _____ Arrive _____

Accommodation _____

_____

Depart _____ Arrive _____

Accommodation _____

_____

Depart _____ Arrive _____

Accommodation _____

_____

_____

_____

# ▪ I T I N E R A R Y ▪

Depart _____ Arrive _____

Accommodation _____

_____

Depart _____ Arrive _____

Accommodation _____

_____

Depart _____ Arrive _____

Accommodation _____

_____

Depart _____ Arrive _____

Accommodation _____

_____

Depart _____ Arrive _____

Accommodation _____

_____

Depart _____ Arrive _____

Accommodation _____

_____

Depart _____ Arrive _____

Accommodation _____

_____

_____

_____

# ■ P L A N N I N G    N O T E S ■

Hotels _____

_____

_____

_____

_____

_____

_____

_____

Restaurants _____

_____

_____

_____

_____

_____

_____

Museums _____

_____

_____

_____

_____

_____

_____

# ■ P L A N N I N G　　N O T E S ■

Special places _____

_____

_____

_____

_____

_____

_____

_____

Special events _____

_____

_____

_____

_____

_____

_____

_____

People to contact _____

_____

_____

_____

_____

_____

_____

## ■ P O S T C A R D  L I S T ■

Name _____

Address _____

_____

Name _____

Address _____

_____

Name _____

Address _____

_____

Name _____

Address _____

_____

Name _____

Address _____

_____

Name _____

Address _____

_____

Name _____

Address _____

_____

Name _____

Address _____

■

# ■ P O S T C A R D   L I S T ■

Name _____

Address _____

_____

Name _____

Address _____

_____

Name _____

Address _____

_____

Name _____

Address _____

_____

Name _____

Address _____

_____

Name _____

Address _____

_____

Name _____

Address _____

_____

Name _____

Address _____

## ■ T R A V E L L E R ' S ■

## ■ C H E Q U E S ■

| Number | Amount | Date & place cashed | Exchange rate |
|--------|--------|---------------------|---------------|
|        |        |                     |               |

# ■ T R A V E L L E R ' S ■
# ■ C H E Q U E S ■

| Number | Amount | Date & place cashed | Exchange rate |
| --- | --- | --- | --- |
| | | | |

# ■ A T M ■
## ■ W I T H D R A W A L S ■

| Date | City | Bank | Withdrawal amount | Currency |
|------|------|------|-------------------|----------|
|      |      |      |                   |          |

# ■ A T M ■
## ■ W I T H D R A W A L S ■

| Date | City | Bank | Withdrawal amount | Currency |
|------|------|------|-------------------|----------|
|      |      |      |                   |          |

# ■ E X P E N S E S ■

| Item | Amount | Day/place bought | Method of payment |
|------|--------|------------------|-------------------|
|      |        |                  |                   |
|      |        |                  |                   |
|      |        |                  |                   |
|      |        |                  |                   |
|      |        |                  |                   |
|      |        |                  |                   |
|      |        |                  |                   |
|      |        |                  |                   |
|      |        |                  |                   |
|      |        |                  |                   |
|      |        |                  |                   |
|      |        |                  |                   |
|      |        |                  |                   |
|      |        |                  |                   |
|      |        |                  |                   |
|      |        |                  |                   |
|      |        |                  |                   |

# ■ E X P E N S E S ■

| Item | Amount | Day/place bought | Method of payment |
| --- | --- | --- | --- |
| | | | |
| | | | |
| | | | |
| | | | |
| | | | |
| | | | |
| | | | |
| | | | |
| | | | |
| | | | |
| | | | |
| | | | |
| | | | |
| | | | |
| | | | |
| | | | |
| | | | |
| | | | |
| | | | |
| | | | |
| | | | |

# ■ E X P E N S E S ■

| Item | Amount | Day/place bought | Method of payment |
|------|--------|------------------|-------------------|
|      |        |                  |                   |

# ■ E X P E N S E S ■

| Item | Amount | Day/place bought | Method of payment |
|------|--------|------------------|-------------------|
|      |        |                  |                   |
|      |        |                  |                   |
|      |        |                  |                   |
|      |        |                  |                   |
|      |        |                  |                   |
|      |        |                  |                   |
|      |        |                  |                   |
|      |        |                  |                   |
|      |        |                  |                   |
|      |        |                  |                   |
|      |        |                  |                   |

## ■ G I F T S   T O ■
## ■ B R I N G   B A C K ■

■ Person       ■ Item       ■ Price

_____

_____

_____

_____

_____

_____

_____

_____

_____

_____

_____

_____

_____

_____

_____

_____

_____

_____

_____

_____

_____

# ■ A D D R E S S E S ■

Name ——————————————————————————

Address ——————————————————————————

————————————————————————————————

Telephone ———————————— E-mail ————————————

Name ——————————————————————————

Address ——————————————————————————

————————————————————————————————

Telephone ———————————— E-mail ————————————

Name ——————————————————————————

Address ——————————————————————————

————————————————————————————————

Telephone ———————————— E-mail ————————————

Name ——————————————————————————

Address ——————————————————————————

————————————————————————————————

Telephone ———————————— E-mail ————————————

Name ——————————————————————————

Address ——————————————————————————

————————————————————————————————

Telephone ———————————— E-mail ————————————

# ■ A D D R E S S E S ■

Name _____

Address _____

_____

Telephone _____ E-mail _____

Name _____

Address _____

_____

Telephone _____ E-mail _____

Name _____

Address _____

_____

Telephone _____ E-mail _____

Name _____

Address _____

_____

Telephone _____ E-mail _____

Name _____

Address _____

_____

Telephone _____ E-mail _____

# ■ A D D R E S S E S ■

Name ——————————————————————

Address ——————————————————————

——————————————————————

Telephone ———————————— E-mail ——————————

Name ——————————————————————

Address ——————————————————————

——————————————————————

Telephone ———————————— E-mail ——————————

Name ——————————————————————

Address ——————————————————————

——————————————————————

Telephone ———————————— E-mail ——————————

Name ——————————————————————

Address ——————————————————————

——————————————————————

Telephone ———————————— E-mail ——————————

Name ——————————————————————

Address ——————————————————————

——————————————————————

Telephone ———————————— E-mail ——————————

# ■ A D D R E S S E S ■

Name _____

Address _____

_____

Telephone _____ E-mail _____

Name _____

Address _____

_____

Telephone _____ E-mail _____

Name _____

Address _____

_____

Telephone _____ E-mail _____

Name _____

Address _____

_____

Telephone _____ E-mail _____

Name _____

Address _____

_____

Telephone _____ E-mail _____

■

■

■

■ D A T E ■ ■

74
■

■

■ D A T E ■

■

■

■

# ■ C L O T H I N G   S I Z E S ■

## WOMEN'S CLOTHING

DRESSES, SUITS, COATS, SWEATERS, ETC.

| Australia/UK | 10 | 12 | 14 | 16 | 18 | 20 |
|---|---|---|---|---|---|---|
| United States | 8 | 10 | 12 | 14 | 16 | 18 |
| France | 38 | 40 | 42 | 44 | 46 | |
| Germany | 36 | 38 | 40 | 42 | 44 | 46 |
| Italy | 42 | 44 | 46 | 48 | 50 | 52 |

PANTYHOSE

| Australia | | | S | M | L | XL | | |
|---|---|---|---|---|---|---|---|---|
| USA/UK | 8 | 8½ | 9 | 9½ | 10 | 10½ | 11 | 11½ |
| Continent | 35 | 36 | 37 | 38 | 39 | 40 | 41 | 42 |
| France/Germany | 0 | 1 | 2 | 3 | 4 | 5 | 6 | 7 |

SHOES

| B Fitting | 5 | 5½ | 6 | 6½ | 7 | 7½ | 8 | 8½ | 9 | 9½ | 10 |
|---|---|---|---|---|---|---|---|---|---|---|---|
| United Kingdom | 3 | 3½ | 4 | 4½ | 5 | 5½ | 6 | 6½ | 7 | 7½ | 8 |
| Continent | 35 | 35½ | 36 | 36½ | 37 | 37½ | 38 | 38½ | 39 | 39½ | 40 |

## MEN'S CLOTHING

SUITS, JACKETS

| Australia | 92 | 94 | 96 | 100 | 102 | 104 | 106 | 108 | 112 |
|---|---|---|---|---|---|---|---|---|---|
| USA/UK | 36 | 37 | 38 | 39 | 40 | 41 | 42 | 43 | 44 |
| Continent | 46 | | 48 | | 50 | | 54 | | 56 |

SWEATERS

| Australia | 14 | 16 | 18 | 20 | 22 | 24 | 26 |
|---|---|---|---|---|---|---|---|
| USA/UK | 36 | 38 | 40 | 42 | 44 | 46 | 48 |
| Continent | 46 | 48 | 50 | 52 | 54 | 56 | 58 |

SHIRTS

| Australia/Contin. | 37 | 38 | 39 | 40 | 41 | 42 | 43 | 44 | 46 |
|---|---|---|---|---|---|---|---|---|---|
| USA/UK | 14½ | 15 | 15½ | 15¾ | 16 | 16½ | 17 | 17½ | 18 |

SHOES

| Australia/UK | 6 | 7 | 8 | 9 | 10 | 11 | 12 |
|---|---|---|---|---|---|---|---|
| United States | 7 | 8 | 9 | 10 | 11 | 12 | 13 |
| Continent | 40 | 41 | 42 | 43 | 44 | 45 | 46 |

# ■ W O R L D   C U R R E N C I E S ■

# ■ A N D   L A N G U A G E S ■

| Country | Currency | Official language(s) |
|---|---|---|
| Afghanistan | Afghani = 100 puls | Persian, Pushtu |
| Albania | Lek = 100 qindars | Albanian |
| Algeria | Dinar = 100 centimes | Arabic |
| Andorra | French franc = 100 centimes; Spanish peseta = 100 centimos | Catalan |
| Angola | Kwanza = 100 lwei | Portuguese |
| Antigua & Barbuda | EC dollar = 100 cents | English |
| Argentina | Peso = 100 centavos | Spanish |
| Armenia | Dram = 100 louma | Armenian |
| Australia | Dollar = 100 cents | English |
| Austria | EURO = 100 cents | German |
| Azerbaijan | Manat = 100 gopik | Azerbaijani |
| Bahamas | Dollar = 100 cents | English |
| Bahrain | Dinar = 1000 fils | Arabic |
| Bangladesh | Taka = 100 paisa | Bangla |
| Barbados | Dollar = 100 cents | English |
| Belarus | Rouble = 100 kopeks | Belarusian |
| Belgium | EURO = 100 cents | French, Dutch |
| Belize | Dollar = 100 cents | English |
| Bermuda | Dollar = 100 cents | English |
| Bhutan | Ngultrum = 100 chetrum | Dzongkha |
| Bolivia | Boliviano = 100 cents | Spanish, Quechua, Aymará |
| Bosnia & Herzegovina | KM (convertible mark) | Bosnian |
| Botswana | Pula = 100 thebe | English |
| Brazil | Real = 100 centavos | Portuguese |
| Brunei | Dollar = 100 cents | Malay |
| Bulgaria | Lev = 100 stotinki | Bulgarian |
| Burundi | Franc = 100 centimes | Kirundi, French |
| Cambodia | Riel = 100 sen | Khmer |
| Cameroon | CFA franc = 100 centimes | French, English |
| Canada | Dollar = 100 cents | English, French |
| Central African Republic | CFA franc = 100 centimes | French |

| | | |
|---|---|---|
| Chad | CFA franc = 100 centimes | French |
| Chile | Peso = 100 centavos | Spanish |
| China | Yuan RMB = 10 jiao = 100 fen | Mandarin |
| Colombia | Peso = 100 centavos | Spanish |
| Congo | CFA franc = 100 centimes | French |
| Congo, Democratic Rep. of the (formerly Zaire) | Zaire = 100 makuta | French |
| Costa Rica | Colón = 100 centimos | Spanish |
| Côte d'Ivoire | CFA franc = 100 centimes | French |
| Croatia | Kuna = 100 lipa | Croatian |
| Cuba | Peso = 100 centavos | Spanish |
| Cyprus | Pound = 100 cents | Greek |
| Czech Republic | Koruna = 100 haleru | Czech |
| Denmark | Krone = 100 øre | Danish |
| Djibouti | Franc = 100 centimes | Arabic, French |
| Dominican Republic | Peso = 100 centavos | Spanish |
| Ecuador | Sucre = 100 centavos | Spanish, Quechua |
| Egypt | Pound = 100 piastres | Arabic |
| El Salvador | Colón = 100 centavos | Spanish |
| Eritrea | Ethiopian birr = 100 cents | Tigrinya, Arabic |
| Estonia | Kroon = 100 cents | Estonian |
| Ethiopia | Birr = 100 cents | Amharic |
| Fiji | Dollar = 100 cents | English, Fijian |
| Finland | EURO = 100 cents | Finnish |
| France | EURO = 100 cents | French |
| French Guiana | French franc = 100 centimes | French |
| French Polynesia | CFP franc = 100 centimes | French |
| Gambia | Dalasi = 100 bututs | English |
| Georgia | Lari = 100 cents | Georgian |
| Germany | EURO = 100 cents | German |
| Ghana | Cedi = 100 pesewas | English |
| Gibraltar | Pound = 100 pence | English |
| Greece | EURO = 100 cents | Greek |
| Greenland | Danish krone = 100 ore | Danish |
| Grenada | EC dollar = 100 cents | English |
| Guatemala | Quetzal = 100 centavos | Spanish |
| Guinea | Franc = 100 centimes | French |
| Guyana | Dollar = 100 cents | English |
| Haiti | Gourde = 100 centimes | French, French Creole |
| Honduras | Lempira = 100 centavos | Spanish |
| Hong Kong | Dollar = 100 cents | Mandarin |

| Country | Currency | Language |
|---|---|---|
| Hungary | Forint = 100 filler | Hungarian |
| Iceland | Krona = 100 aurar | Icelandic |
| India | Rupee = 100 paisa | Hindi, English |
| Indonesia | Rupiah = 100 sen | Bahasa Indonesia |
| Iran | Rial = 100 dinars | Farsi |
| Iraq | Dinar = 1000 fils | Arabic |
| Ireland (Eire) | EURO = 100 cents | Gaelic Irish, English |
| Israel | Shekel = 100 agorat | Hebrew |
| Italy | EURO = 100 cents | Italian |
| Jamaica | Dollar = 100 cents | English |
| Japan | Yen = 100 sen | Japanese |
| Jordan | Dinar = 1000 fils | Arabic |
| Kazakhstan | Tenge = 100 tein | Kazakh |
| Kenya | Shilling = 100 cents | Swahili |
| Kiribati | Australian dollar = 100 cents | English |
| Kuwait | Dinar = 1000 fils | Arabic |
| Laos | Kip = 100 att | Lao |
| Latvia | Lats = 100 santimi | Latvian |
| Lebanon | Pound = 100 piastres | Arabic |
| Lesotho | Loti = 100 lisente | Sesotho, English |
| Liberia | Dollar = 100 cents | English |
| Libya | Dinar = 1000 dirhams | Arabic |
| Liechtenstein | Swiss franc = 100 centimes | German |
| Lithuania | Litas = 100 centas | Lithuania |
| Luxembourg | EURO = 100 cents | Letzeburgish, French, German |
| Macedonia | Denar = 100 deni | Macedonian, Serbo-Croatian (no official language) |
| Madagascar | Franc = 100 centimes | Malagasy, French |
| Malawi | Kwacha = 100 tambala | English, Chewa |
| Malaysia | Ringgit = 100 cents | Malay, Chinese |
| Maldives | Rufiyaa (rupee) = 100 laari | Divehi |
| Mali | CFA franc = 100 centimes | French |
| Malta | Lira = 100 cents | Maltese |
| Mauritania | Ouguiya = 5 khoums | French |
| Mauritius | Rupee = 100 cents | English |
| Mexico | Peso = 100 centavos | Spanish |
| Micronesia | US dollar = 100 cents | English |
| Moldova | Leu = 100 bani | Moldavian |
| Monaco | EURO = 100 cents | French |

| Mongolia | Tugrik = 100 möngös | Khalkha Mongol |
| Montserrat | EC dollar = 100 cents | English |
| Morocco | Dirham = 100 centimes | Arabic |
| Mozambique | Metical = 100 centavos | Portuguese |
| Myanmar (Burma) | Kyat = 100 pyas | Burmese |
| Namibia | Dollar = 100 cents | English |
| Nepal | Rupee = 100 paisa | Nepali |
| Netherlands | EURO = 100 cents | Dutch |
| New Caledonia | CFP franc = 100 centimes | French |
| New Zealand | Dollar = 100 cents | English |
| Nicaragua | Córdoba = 100 centavos | Spanish |
| Niger | CFA franc = 100 centimes | French |
| Nigeria | Naira = 100 kobo | English |
| North Korea | Won = 100 chon | Korean |
| Norway | Krone = 100 øre | Bokmal, Nynorsk |
| Oman | Rial = 1000 baizas | Arabic |
| Pakistan | Rupee = 100 paisa | Urdu |
| Panama | Balboa = 100 centesimos | Spanish |
| Papua New Guinea | Kina = 100 toea | Pidgin English, Motu |
| Paraguay | Guaraní = 100 centimos | Spanish, Guaraní |
| Peru | Sol = 100 centavos | Spanish, Quechua, Aymará |
| Philippines | Peso = 100 centavos | Pilipino, English |
| Poland | Zloty = 100 groszy | Polish |
| Portugal | EURO = 100 cents | Portuguese |
| Puerto Rico | US dollar = 100 cents | English |
| Qatar | Rial = 100 dirhams | Arabic |
| Romania | Leu = 100 bani | Romanian |
| Russian Federation | Rouble = 100 kopeks | Russia |
| Rwanda | Franc = 100 centimes | Kinyarwanda, French |
| San Marino | EURO = 100 cents | Italian |
| Saudi Arabia | Riyal = 100 malalah | Arabic |
| Senegal | CFA franc = 100 centimes | French |
| Seychelles | Rupee = 100 cents | Creole |
| Singapore | Dollar = 100 cents | Malay, Mandarin |
| Slovakia | Koruna = 100 haleru | Slovak |
| Slovenia | Tolar = 100 stotins | Slovene |
| Solomon Islands | Dollar = 100 cents | English |
| Somalia | Shilling = 100 cents | Somali, Arabic |
| South Africa | Rand = 100 cents | Afrikaans |
| South Korea | Won = 100 cents | Korean |

| Spain | EURO = 100 cents | Castilian Spanish, Catalan, Galician, Basque |
|---|---|---|
| Sri Lanka | Rupee = 100 cents | Sinhala |
| Sudan | Pound = 100 piastres | Arabic |
| Suriname | Guilder = 100 cents | Dutch |
| Swaziland | Lilangeni = 100 cents | Siswati, English |
| Sweden | Krona = 100 öre | Swedish |
| Switzerland | Franc = 100 centimes | German, French, Italian, Romansch |
| Syria | Pound = 100 piastres | Arabic |
| Taiwan | New dollar = 100 cents | Mandarin |
| Tanzania | Shilling = 100 seneti | Swahili, English |
| Thailand | Baht = 100 satangs | Thai |
| Tonga | Pa'anga = 100 seneti | Tongan |
| Trinidad & Tobago | Dollar = 100 cents | English |
| Tunisia | Dinar = 1000 millimes | Arabic |
| Turkey | Lira = 100 kurus | Turkish |
| Uganda | Shilling = 100 cents | English |
| Ukraine | Hryvnia = 100 cents | Ukrainian |
| United Arab Emirates | Dirham = 100 fils | Arabic |
| United Kingdom | Pound = 100 pence | English |
| United States of America | Dollar = 100 cents | English |
| Uruguay | Nuevo peso = 100 centésimos | Spanish |
| Vanuatu | Vatu = 100 centimes | Bislama, English, French |
| Venezuela | Bolívar = 100 centimos | Spanish |
| Vietnam | Dông = 10 háo = 100 Xu | Vietnamese |
| Western Samoa | Tala = 100 sene | Samoan, English |
| Yemen | Rial = 100 fils; Dinar = 1000 fils | Arabic |
| Yugoslavia | New dinar = 100 para | Serbian |
| Zambia | Kwacha = 100 ngwee | English |
| Zimbabwe | Dollar = 100 cents | English |

# ▪ W O R L D  C L I M A T E ▪

| City | T = mean daily temperature °C | | | R = mean monthly rainfall in mm | | |
|------|------|------|------|------|------|------|
| Country | JAN | FEB | MAR | APR | MAY | JUN |
| | T(°C) | T(°C) | T(°C) | T(°C) | T(°C) | T(°C) |
| | R(mm) | R(mm) | R(mm) | R(mm) | R(mm) | R(mm) |
| Auckland | 20.0 | 20.5 | 19.4 | 17.1 | 14.5 | 12.3 |
| New Zealand | 43.9 | 116.9 | 87.1 | 130.5 | 130.2 | 118.6 |
| Bahrain | 17.4 | 18.3 | 21.2 | 25.6 | 29.6 | 32.0 |
| | 16 | 15 | 11 | 6 | 1 | 0 |
| Bangkok | 26.1 | 27.6 | 29.2 | 30.3 | 29.8 | 28.9 |
| Thailand | 9 | 29 | 34 | 89 | 166 | 171 |
| Beirut | 13.9 | 14.1 | 15.3 | 18.1 | 21.0 | 24.1 |
| Lebanon | 113 | 80 | 77 | 26 | 10 | 1 |
| Bombay | 24.3 | 24.9 | 26.9 | 28.7 | 29.9 | 29.1 |
| India | 2 | 1 | 0 | 3 | 16 | 520 |
| Brisbane | 25.0 | 24.7 | 23.6 | 21.2 | 18.2 | 15.8 |
| Australia | 14.3 | 183 | 147 | 78 | 57 | 56 |
| Buenos Aires | 23.4 | 22.2 | 20.2 | 16.2 | 12.9 | 10 |
| Argentina | 105.4 | 93.8 | 100 | 90.4 | 80.5 | 55.5 |
| Cairo | 13.8 | 15.2 | 17.4 | 21.1 | 24.7 | 26.9 |
| Egypt | 3.4 | 4.7 | 1.1 | 0.5 | 0.7 | 0.4 |
| Chicago | -3.3 | -2.3 | 2.4 | 9.5 | 15.6 | 21.5 |
| United States | 47 | 41 | 70 | 77 | 95 | 103 |
| Darwin | 28.2 | 27.9 | 28.3 | 28.2 | 26.8 | 25.4 |
| Australia | 341 | 338 | 274 | 121 | 9 | 1 |
| Delhi | 14.3 | 17.3 | 22.9 | 29.1 | 33.5 | 34.5 |
| India | 25 | 22 | 17 | 7 | 8 | 65 |
| Frankfurt | 0.0 | 1.0 | 5.0 | 9.4 | 13.8 | 17.1 |
| Germany | 57 | 44 | 36 | 43 | 54 | 72 |
| Hong Kong | 15.4 | 15.8 | 18.2 | 21.8 | 25.6 | 27.5 |
| | 30 | 60 | 70 | 133 | 332 | 479 |
| Honolulu | 22.5 | 22.4 | 22.7 | 23.4 | 24.4 | 25.5 |
| United States | 96 | 84 | 73 | 33 | 25 | 8 |
| Johannesburg | 19.7 | 19.5 | 18.6 | 16.5 | 13.4 | 10.6 |
| South Africa | 120.5 | 138.0 | 86.0 | 62.1 | 31.6 | 6.8 |
| Karachi | 18.9 | 21.2 | 24.3 | 26.9 | 29.2 | 30.4 |
| Pakistan | 7 | 11 | 6 | 2 | 0 | 7 |
| Kuala Lumpur | 26.2 | 26.6 | 26.9 | 26.9 | 27.3 | 26.8 |
| Malaysia | 176.6 | 112.6 | 206.9 | 308.7 | 218.1 | 145.5 |

| JUL | AUG | SEP | OCT | NOV | DEC | YEAR |
|---|---|---|---|---|---|---|
| T(°C) | T(°C) | T(°C) | T(°C) | T(°C) | T(°C) | T(°C) |
| R(mm) | R(mm) | R(mm) | R(mm) | R(mm) | R(mm) | R(mm) |
| 11.0 | 11.9 | 13.3 | 15.1 | 17.0 | 18.5 | 15.9 |
| 136.9 | 141.5 | 92.9 | 110.8 | 84.9 | 95.3 | 1289.5 |
| 33.8 | 34.3 | 32.5 | 29.0 | 24.5 | 19.2 | 26.4 |
| 0 | 0 | 0 | 0 | 9 | 18 | 76 |
| 28.4 | 28.2 | 27.9 | 27.6 | 26.7 | 25.5 | 28.0 |
| 178 | 191 | 306 | 255 | 57 | 7 | 1492 |
| 26.2 | 27.1 | 25.7 | 23.0 | 18.8 | 15.5 | 20.2 |
| 0 | 0 | 7 | 20 | 78 | 105 | 517 |
| 27.5 | 27.1 | 27.4 | 28.3 | 27.5 | 25.9 | 27.3 |
| 709 | 419 | 297 | 88 | 21 | 2 | 2078 |
| 15.0 | 16.1 | 18.1 | 20.7 | 22.5 | 24.3 | 20.4 |
| 49 | 30 | 45 | 77 | 92 | 136 | 1092 |
| 9.8 | 10.9 | 13 | 15.9 | 18.9 | 21.8 | 16.3 |
| 57.7 | 53.7 | 60.9 | 98.7 | 91.1 | 88.8 | 976.5 |
| 28.0 | 28.0 | 26.0 | 23.7 | 19.3 | 15.3 | 21.6 |
| 0 | 0 | 0 | 0.1 | 2.7 | 11.0 | 24.6 |
| 24.3 | 23.6 | 19.1 | 13.0 | 4.4 | -1.6 | 10.5 |
| 86 | 80 | 69 | 71 | 56 | 48 | 843 |
| 25.1 | 25.8 | 27.7 | 29.1 | 29.2 | 28.7 | 27.6 |
| 2 | 5 | 17 | 66 | 156 | 233 | 1562 |
| 31.2 | 29.9 | 29.3 | 25.9 | 20.2 | 15.7 | 25.3 |
| 211 | 173 | 150 | 31 | 1 | 5 | 715 |
| 18.7 | 17.9 | 14.5 | 9.2 | 4.8 | 1.2 | 9.4 |
| 68 | 77 | 56 | 50 | 53 | 53 | 663 |
| 28.4 | 27.9 | 27.3 | 24.7 | 21.2 | 17.4 | 22.6 |
| 286 | 415 | 364 | 33 | 46 | 17 | 2265 |
| 26.0 | 26.3 | 26.2 | 25.7 | 24.4 | 23.1 | 24.4 |
| 11 | 23 | 25 | 47 | 55 | 76 | 556 |
| 10.8 | 13.3 | 15.7 | 18.5 | 18.8 | 19.2 | 16.2 |
| 15.4 | 6.8 | 30.6 | 64.8 | 126.4 | 131.6 | 820.6 |
| 29.3 | 28.2 | 27.6 | 27.1 | 24.9 | 21.3 | 25.8 |
| 96 | 50 | 15 | 2 | 2 | 6 | 204 |
| 26.5 | 26.4 | 26.3 | 26.1 | 26.1 | 26.0 | 26.5 |
| 156.7 | 156.7 | 186.0 | 292.9 | 290.7 | 251.4 | 2502.8 |

# ▪ W O R L D   C L I M A T E ▪

| City Country | JAN | FEB | MAR | APR | MAY | JUN |
|---|---|---|---|---|---|---|
| | T(°C) R(mm) | T(°C) R(mm) | T(°C) R(mm) | T(°C) R(mm) | T(°C) R(mm) | T(°C) R(mm) |
| London | 3.2 | 3.7 | 5.5 | 8.1 | 11.2 | 14.5 |
| United Kingdom | 69.9 | 49.3 | 50.8 | 67.2 | 58.2 | 52.8 |
| Los Angeles | 13.2 | 13.9 | 15.2 | 16.6 | 18.2 | 20.0 |
| United States | 78 | 85 | 57 | 30 | 4 | 2 |
| Manila | 25.4 | 26.1 | 27.2 | 28.9 | 29.4 | 28.5 |
| Philippines | 18 | 7 | 6 | 24 | 110 | 236 |
| Mexico City | 21 | 22 | 24 | 25 | 26 | 24 |
| Mexico | 7 | 5 | 12 | 20 | 48 | 106 |
| Montreal | -8.9 | -7.6 | -1.4 | 6.7 | 13.6 | 19.1 |
| Canada | 80 | 71 | 75 | 77 | 75 | 87 |
| Moscow | -11.0 | -8.8 | -3.4 | 5.6 | 13.2 | 16.3 |
| Russia | 40.5 | 38.7 | 38.5 | 40.7 | 46.6 | 60.7 |
| Nairobi | 20.1 | 20.5 | 21.0 | 20.5 | 19.5 | 18.1 |
| Kenya | 53.2 | 25.6 | 86.1 | 167.9 | 145.2 | 40.3 |
| New York | 0.7 | 0.8 | 4.7 | 10.8 | 16.9 | 21.9 |
| United States | 84 | 72 | 102 | 87 | 93 | 84 |
| Rome | 7.9 | 8.9 | 10.8 | 13.7 | 17.4 | 21.4 |
| Italy | 81.9 | 70.4 | 54.6 | 44.0 | 42.6 | 17.8 |
| Singapore | 26.1 | 26.7 | 27.2 | 27.6 | 27.8 | 28.0 |
| | 285 | 164 | 154 | 160 | 131 | 177 |
| Sydney | 21.9 | 21.9 | 21.2 | 18.3 | 15.7 | 13.1 |
| Australia | 104 | 125 | 129 | 101 | 115 | 141 |
| Tehran | 3.5 | 5.2 | 10.2 | 15.4 | 21.2 | 26.1 |
| Iran | 37 | 23 | 36 | 31 | 14 | 2 |
| Tel Aviv | 13.6 | 14.0 | 15.4 | 17.9 | 20.3 | 23.8 |
| Israel | 124.8 | 68.3 | 50.8 | 18.7 | 1.7 | 0 |
| Tokyo | 3.7 | 4.3 | 7.6 | 13.1 | 17.6 | 21.1 |
| Japan | 48 | 73 | 101 | 135 | 131 | 182 |
| Toronto | -4.4 | -3.8 | 0.6 | 7.6 | 13.2 | 19.2 |
| Canada | 62 | 57 | 66 | 67 | 73 | 63 |
| Washington DC | 2.7 | 3.2 | 7.1 | 13.2 | 18.8 | 23.4 |
| United States | 82 | 70 | 92 | 90 | 103 | 97 |
| Zurich | -1.1 | 0.3 | 4.5 | 8.6 | 12.7 | 15.9 |
| Switzerland | 75 | 70 | 66 | 80 | 107 | 136 |

| JUL | AUG | SEP | OCT | NOV | DEC | YEAR |
|---|---|---|---|---|---|---|
| T(°C) | T(°C) | T(°C) | T(°C) | T(°C) | T(°C) | T(°C) |
| R(mm) | R(mm) | R(mm) | R(mm) | R(mm) | R(mm) | R(mm) |
| 15.9 | 15.6 | 13.9 | 10.9 | 6.4 | 3.4 | 9.4 |
| 57.7 | 62.8 | 80.8 | 62.9 | 90.4 | 73.4 | 776.2 |
| 22.8 | 22.8 | 22.2 | 19.7 | 17.1 | 14.6 | 18.0 |
| 0 | 1 | 6 | 10 | 27 | 73 | 373 |
| 27.9 | 27.4 | 27.4 | 27.2 | 26.4 | 25.4 | 27.3 |
| 253 | 480 | 271 | 201 | 129 | 56 | 1791 |
| 23 | 23 | 22 | 22 | 22 | 21 | 22.9 |
| 129 | 121 | 109 | 43 | 15 | 7 | 622 |
| 21.6 | 20.4 | 15.8 | 10.1 | 2.9 | -5.7 | 7.2 |
| 93 | 92 | 87 | 79 | 93 | 91 | 999 |
| 18.1 | 16.7 | 11.1 | 5.8 | -1.2 | -6.9 | 4.6 |
| 86.0 | 67.5 | 54.7 | 46.5 | 43.0 | 50.7 | 614.0 |
| 17.0 | 17.5 | 19.0 | 20.1 | 19.7 | 19.6 | 19.4 |
| 18.6 | 12.4 | 30.2 | 39.2 | 123.8 | 68.9 | 811.4 |
| 24.9 | 23.9 | 20.3 | 14.6 | 8.3 | 2.2 | 12.5 |
| 94 | 113 | 98 | 80 | 86 | 83 | 1076 |
| 24.2 | 24.0 | 21.4 | 17.1 | 12.8 | 9.3 | 15.8 |
| 27.0 | 19.7 | 67.4 | 99.6 | 115.8 | 101.4 | 723.9 |
| 27.4 | 27.3 | 27.3 | 27.2 | 26.7 | 26.3 | 27.1 |
| 163 | 200 | 122 | 184 | 236 | 306 | 2282 |
| 12.3 | 13.4 | 15.3 | 17.6 | 19.4 | 21.0 | 17.6 |
| 94 | 83 | 72 | 80 | 77 | 86 | 1205 |
| 29.5 | 28.4 | 24.6 | 18.3 | 10.6 | 4.9 | 16.5 |
| 1 | 1 | 1 | 5 | 29 | 27 | 208 |
| 25.9 | 26.9 | 25.4 | 22.5 | 18.7 | 15.4 | 20.0 |
| 0 | 0 | 3.1 | 10.5 | 103.3 | 153.8 | 535.0 |
| 25.1 | 26.4 | 22.8 | 16.7 | 11.3 | 6.1 | 14.7 |
| 146 | 147 | 217 | 220 | 101 | 61 | 1563 |
| 21.8 | 21.1 | 17.0 | 11.2 | 4.8 | -1.8 | 8.9 |
| 81 | 67 | 61 | 61 | 67 | 64 | 790 |
| 25.7 | 24.7 | 20.9 | 15.0 | 8.7 | 3.4 | 13.9 |
| 107 | 107 | 101 | 83 | 78 | 77 | 1087 |
| 17.6 | 17.0 | 14.0 | 8.6 | 3.7 | 0.1 | 8.5 |
| 143 | 131 | 108 | 80 | 76 | 65 | 1137 |

# ■ W O R L D   T I M E ■

## ■ Z O N E S ■

Time around the world when it is 12 noon at the Greenwich Meridian.

•Oslo

•Stockholm

•London  •Moscow

•Frankfurt

•Paris

Montreal•          •Rome

•Madrid

Boston•

Chicago•

New York•          •Beirut          •Delhi

Los Angeles•                         •Jeddah          •Tokyo

•Kuwait          •Hong Kong

•Bombay

•Bangkok

•Manila

Mexico City•     Accra•          •Kuala Lumpur

•Singapore

•Nairobi          •Jakarta

Lima•

Rio de Janeiro•

Santiago de Chile•          •Johannesburg          •Sydney

Buenos Aires•          •Perth

Melbourne•

Auckland•

| 0 | 1 | 2 | 3 | 4 | 5 | 6 | 7 | 8 | 9 | 10 | 11 | 12 | 13 | 14 | 15 | 16 | 17 | 18 | 19 | 20 | 21 | 22 | 23 | 24 |
|---|---|---|---|---|---|---|---|---|---|----|----|----|----|----|----|----|----|----|----|----|----|----|----|----|
| -12 | -11 | -10 | -9 | -8 | -7 | -6 | -5 | -4 | -3 | -2 | -1 | **GMT** | +1 | +2 | +3 | +4 | +5 | +6 | +7 | +8 | +9 | +10 | +11 | +12 |

# ■ FOREIGN PHRASES ■

## ■ SOME BASIC ■

| ENGLISH | FRENCH | ITALIAN | SPANISH | GERMAN | JAPANESE |
|---|---|---|---|---|---|
| Hello | Bonjour | Buon giorno | Buenos días | Guten tag | Kon-nichiwa |
| Goodbye | Au revoir | Arrivederci | Adios | Auf Wiedersehn | Sayonara |
| Please | S'il vous plait | Per favore | Por favor | Bitte | Doozo |
| Thank you | Merci | Grazie | Gracias | Danke | Domo arigato |
| How much? | Combien? | Quanto? | ¿Cuánto? | Wieviel? | Ikura desu ka? |
| Yes | Oui | Si | Si | Ja | Hai |
| No | Non | No | No | Nein | I-ie |
| I don't understand | Je ne comprends pas | Non capisco | No entiendo | Ich verstehe nicht | Wakarimasen |
| One | Un | Uno | Uno | Eins | Ichi |
| Two | Deux | Due | Dos | Zwei | Ni |
| Three | Trois | Tre | Tres | Drei | San |
| Four | Quatre | Quattro | Cuatro | Vier | Shi |
| Five | Cinq | Cinque | Cinco | Fünf | Go |
| Six | Six | Sei | Seis | Sechs | Roku |
| Seven | Sept | Sette | Siete | Sieben | Shichi |
| Eight | Huit | Otto | Ocho | Acht | Hachi |
| Nine | Neuf | Nove | Nueve | Neun | Kyuu |
| Ten | Dix | Dieci | Diez | Zehn | Juu |

# ■ I N T E R N A T I O N A L ■
# ■ D I A L L I N G    C O D E S ■

| COUNTRY | IDD ACCESS CODE(S) | IDD COUNTRY CODE |
|---|---|---|
| Afghanistan | 00 | 93 |
| Albania | 00 | 355 |
| Algeria | 00 | 213 |
| Angola | 01 | 244 |
| Argentina | 00 | 54 |
| Armenia | 810 | 374 |
| Australia | 0011 | 61 |
| Austria | 00, 900 (Vienna) | 43 |
| Bahamas | 011 | 1+242 |
| Bahrain | 0 | 973 |
| Bangladesh | 00 | 880 |
| Barbados | 011 | 1+246 |
| Belarus | 810 | 375 |
| Belgium | 00 | 32 |
| Belize | 00 | 501 |
| Bermuda | 011 | 1+441 |
| Bolivia | 0 | 591 |
| Bosnia & Herzegovina | 011 | 387 |
| Botswana | 00 | 267 |
| Brazil | 00 | 55 |
| Brunei | 01 | 673 |
| Bulgaria | 00 | 359 |
| Cambodia | 00 | 855 |
| Cameroon | 00 | 237 |
| Canada | 011 | 1 |
| Chad | 15 | 235 |
| Chile | 00 | 56 |
| China | 00 | 86 |
| Colombia | 90 | 57 |
| Congo | 00 | 242 |
| Congo, Democratic Rep. of the | 00 | 243 |
| Costa Rica | 00 | 506 |
| Côte d'Ivoire | 00 | 225 |

| COUNTRY | IDD ACCESS CODE(S) | IDD COUNTRY CODE |
|---|---|---|
| Croatia | 99 | 385 |
| Cuba | 119 | 53 |
| Cyprus | 00 | 357 |
| Czech Republic | 00 | 420 |
| Denmark | 00 | 45 |
| Ecuador | 0 | 593 |
| Egypt | 00 | 20 |
| Estonia | 800 | 372 |
| Ethiopia | 00 | 251 |
| Fiji | 05 | 679 |
| Finland | 00 | 358 |
| France | 00 | 33 |
| Gambia | 00 | 220 |
| Georgia | 810 | 995 |
| Germany | 00 | 49 |
| Ghana | 00 | 233 |
| Gibraltar | 00 | 350 |
| Greece | 00 | 30 |
| Grenada | 001 | 1+809 |
| Guatemala | 00 | 502 |
| Guyana | 001 | 592 |
| Haiti | 00 | 509 |
| Honduras | 00 | 504 |
| Hong Kong | 001 | 852 |
| Hungary | 00 | 36 |
| Iceland | 00 | 354 |
| India | 00 | 91 |
| Indonesia | 001, 008 | 62 |
| Ireland (Eire) | 00 | 353 |
| Israel | 00 | 972 |
| Italy | 00 | 39 |
| Jamaica | 011 | 1+876 |
| Japan | 001 | 81 |
| Jordan | 00 | 962 |
| Kazakhstan | 00 | 7 |
| Kenya | 00 | 254 |
| Laos | 00 | 856 |
| Latvia | 110 | 371 |
| Lebanon | 00 | 961 |
| Lesotho | 00 | 266 |

# ■ I N T E R N A T I O N A L ■
# ■ D I A L L I N G   C O D E S ■

| COUNTRY | IDD ACCESS CODE(S) | IDD COUNTRY CODE |
|---|---|---|
| Liberia | 00 | 231 |
| Liechtenstein | 00 | 41+75 |
| Lithuania | 810 | 370 |
| Luxembourg | 00 | 352 |
| Macau | 00 | 853 |
| Macedonia | 99 | 389 |
| Madagascar | 16 | 261 |
| Malaysia | 00 | 60 |
| Malta | 00 | 356 |
| Mauritius | 00 | 230 |
| Mexico | 98 | 52 |
| Micronesia | 011 | 691 |
| Monaco | 19 | 377 |
| Mongolia | *no access code* | 976 |
| Morocco | 00 | 212 |
| Mozambique | 00 | 258 |
| Myanmar (Burma) | 00 | 95 |
| Nepal | 00 | 977 |
| Netherlands | 00 | 31 |
| New Zealand | 00 | 64 |
| Nicaragua | 00 | 505 |
| Nigeria | 009 | 234 |
| North Korea | 800 | 850 |
| Norway | 00 | 47 |
| Oman | 00 | 968 |
| Pakistan | 00 | 92 |
| Panama | 00 | 507 |
| Papua New Guinea | 05 | 675 |
| Paraguay | 002 | 595 |
| Peru | 00 | 51 |
| Philippines | 00 | 63 |
| Poland | 00 | 48 |

| COUNTRY | IDD ACCESS CODE(S) | IDD COUNTRY CODE |
|---|---|---|
| Portugal | 00, 097 (Lisbon) | 351 |
| Romania | 00 | 40 |
| Russian Federation | 8 | 107 |
| Rwanda | 00 | 250 |
| Saudi Arabia | 00 | 966 |
| Senegal | 00112 | 221 |
| Seychelles | 00 | 248 |
| Singapore | 001 | 65 |
| Slovakia | 00 | 421 |
| Solomon Islands | 00 | 677 |
| Somalia | 16 | 252 |
| South Africa | 09 | 27 |
| South Korea | 001, 002 | 82 |
| Spain | 07 | 34 |
| Sri Lanka | 00 | 94 |
| Sudan | 00 | 249 |
| Swaziland | 0 | 268 |
| Sweden | 009 | 46 |
| Switzerland | 00 | 41 |
| Syria | 00 | 963 |
| Taiwan | 002 | 886 |
| Tanzania | 00 | 255 |
| Thailand | 001 | 66 |
| Trinidad & Tobago | 01 | 1 |
| Tunisia | 00 | 216 |
| Turkey | 00 | 90 |
| Uganda | 00 | 256 |
| Ukraine | 810 | 380 |
| United Arab Emirates | 00 | 971 |
| United Kingdom | 00 | 44 |
| United States Of America | 011 | 1 |
| Uruguay | 00 | 598 |
| Vanuatu | 00 | 678 |
| Venezuela | 00 | 58 |
| Vietnam | 00 | 84 |
| Western Samoa | 0 | 685 |
| Yemen | 00 | 967 |
| Yugoslavia | 99 | 381 |
| Zambia | 00 | 260 |
| Zimbabwe | 110 | 263 |

■

# ■ D I S T A N C E S   F R O M ■
# ■ A I R P O R T S   T O   C I T I E S ■

| COUNTRY | AIRPORT / CODE | DISTANCE |
|---|---|---|
| **AUSTRALIA** | | |
| Melbourne | International / MEL | 19 km |
| Perth | International / PER | 10 km |
| Sydney | Kingsford Smith / SYD | 8 km |
| **AUSTRIA** | | |
| Vienna | Wien (Schwechat) / VIE | 18 km |
| **BELGIUM** | | |
| Brussels | National / BRU | 17 km |
| **CANADA** | | |
| Montreal | Mirabel International / YMX | 55 km |
| Toronto | Lester B. Pearson International / YYZ | 28 km |
| **CHINA** | | |
| Beijing | Capital / PEK | 30 km |
| **FIJI** | | |
| Suva | Nausori / SUV | 23 km |
| **FRANCE** | | |
| Paris | Charles de Gaulle / CDG | 30 km |
| | Orly / ORY | 15 km |
| **GERMANY** | | |
| Berlin | Tegel / BER | 8 km |
| Frankfurt | International (Rhein-Main) / FRA | 12 km |
| Hamburg | Fuhlsbuttel / HAM | 12 km |
| **GREECE** | | |
| Athens | Hellinikon / ATH | 11 km |
| **HONG KONG** | | |
| Hong Kong | International Chek Lap Kok / HKG | 34 km |
| **INDIA** | | |
| New Delhi | International (Palam) / DEL | 14 km |
| **INDONESIA** | | |
| Denpasar | Ngurah Rai / DPS | 13 km |
| Jakartar | Halim Perdana Kusuma Intl. / HLP | 9 km |
| **IRELAND (EIRE)** | | |
| Dublin | Dublin / DUB | 9 km |

■

| COUNTRY | AIRPORT / CODE | DISTANCE |
|---|---|---|
| **ITALY** | | |
| Rome | Leonardo da Vinci (Fiumicino) / FCO | 32 km |
| **JAPAN** | | |
| Osaka | International (Itami) / OSA | 20 km |
| Tokyo | Narita / NRT | 66 km |
| **MALAYSIA** | | |
| Kuala Lumpur | Subang / KUL | 22 km |
| Penang | International (Bayan Lepas) / PEN | 19 km |
| **MEXICO** | | |
| Mexico City | Benito Juarez / MEX | 13 km |
| **NEW ZEALAND** | | |
| Auckland | International / AKL | 22 km |
| Christchurch | International / CHC | 11 km |
| Wellington | International (Rongotai) / WLG | 8 km |
| **PHILIPPINES** | | |
| Manila | Ninoy Aquino International / MNL | 12 km |
| **RUSSIAN FEDERATION** | | |
| Moscow | Sheremetyevo / SVO | 26 km |
| **SINGAPORE** | | |
| Singapore | Singapore Changi / SIN | 20 km |
| **SOUTH AFRICA** | | |
| Johannesburg | International (Jan Smuts) / JNB | 30 km |
| **SPAIN** | | |
| Madrid | Madrid (Barajas) / MAD | 12 km |
| **SWEDEN** | | |
| Stockholm | Arlanda / ARN | 41 km |
| **SWITZERLAND** | | |
| Geneva | Cointrin / GVA | 4 km |
| Zurich | Zurich (Kloten) / ZRH | 11 km |
| **THAILAND** | | |
| Bangkok | International / BKK | 22 km |
| **UNITED KINGDOM** | | |
| London | Gatwick / LGW | 43 km |
| | Heathrow / LHR | 24 km |
| **UNITED STATES** | | |
| Honolulu | International / HNL | 13 km |
| Los Angeles | International / LAX | 24 km |
| New York | JFK International / JFK | 24 km |
| | La Guardia / LGA | 13 km |
| | Newark International / EWR | 27 km |
| San Francisco | International / SFO | 26 km |

# ■ C O N V E R S I O N ■

## ■ C H A R T S ■

OUNCES TO GRAMS
1 oz = 28.3 g
5 oz = 141.5 g
10 oz = 283 g

GRAMS TO OUNCES
1 g = 0.035 oz
5g = 0.176 oz
10 g = 0.353 oz

POUNDS TO KILOGRAMS
1 lb = 0.45 kg
5 lb = 2.27 kg
10 lb = 4.54 kg
50 lb = 22.68 kg
100 lb = 45.36 kg

KILOGRAMS TO POUNDS
1 kg = 2.2 lb
5 kg = 11.02 lb
10 kg = 22.05 lb
50 kg = 110.23 lb
100 kg = 220.46 lb

PINTS TO LITRES
1 pt = 0.57 L
5 pt = 2.84 L
10 pt = 5.68 L

LITRES TO PINTS
1 L = 1.76 pt
5 L = 8.8 pt
10 L = 17.6 pt

GALLONS TO LITRES
1 gal = 4.55 L
5 gal = 22.75 L
10 gal = 45.5 L

LITRES TO GALLONS
1 L = 0.22 gal
5 L = 1.1 gal
10 L = 2.2 gal

INCHES TO CENTIMETRES
1 in = 2.54 cm
5 in = 12.7 cm
10 in = 25.4 cm
50 in = 127 cm

CENTIMETRES TO INCHES
1 cm = 0.39 in
5 cm = 1.97 in
10 cm = 3.94 in
50 cm = 19.7 in

FEET TO METRES
1 ft = 0.30 m
5 ft = 1.52 m
10 ft = 3.05 m
50 ft = 15.2 m
100 ft = 30.4 m

METRES TO FEET
1 m = 3.28 ft
5 m = 16.4 ft
10 m = 32.8 ft
50 m = 164 ft
100 m = 328 ft

■

# ■ C O N V E R S I O N ■
# ■ C H A R T S ■

## YARDS TO METRES
1 yd = 0.91 m
5 yd = 4.57 m
10 yd = 9.14 m
50 yd = 45.72 m
100 yd = 91.44 m

## MILES TO KILOMETRES
1 mile = 1.61 km
5 miles = 8.05 km
10 miles = 16.09 km
50 miles = 80.46 km
100 miles = 160.93 km

## METRES TO YARDS
1 m = 1.09 yd
5 m = 5.47 yd
10 m = 10.94 yd
50 m = 54.68 yd
100 m = 109.36 yd

## KILOMETRES TO MILES
1 km = 0.62 miles
5 km = 31.1 miles
10 km = 6.21 miles
50 km = 31.07 miles
100 km = 62.14 miles

## DEGREES FAHRENHEIT TO DEGREES CELSIUS

| °F | °C |
| --- | --- |
| −40 | −40 |
| 32 | 0 |
| 41 | 5 |
| 50 | 10 |
| 59 | 15 |
| 68 | 20 |
| 86 | 30 |
| 100 | 37.8 |
| 104 | 40 |

# ■ AUSTRALIAN ■
# ■ EMBASSIES ■

*(Under a formal agreement, in countries where no Australian diplomatic office exists, consular services are provided to Australians by Canadian embassies, high commissions or consulates.)*

## ARGENTINA
Australian Embassy
Villanueva 1400
(1426)
BUENOS AIRES
Tel: (1) 777 6580/6585

## ARMENIA
Consulate of Canada
25 Demirjian Street, No. 22
YEREVAN
Tel: (2) 56 7903

## AUSTRIA
Australian Embassy
Mattiellistrasse 2
1040 VIENNA
Tel: (1) 512 8580

## BANGLADESH
Australian High Commission
184 Gulshan Avenue
Gulshan, DHAKA
Tel: (2) 881 3101–5

## BARBADOS
Australian High Commission
Bishop's Court Hill
St Michael, BRIDGETOWN
Tel: (246) 435 2834

## BELGIUM
Australian Embassy
Guimard Centre
Rue Guimard 6–8
1040 BRUSSELS
Tel: 286 0500

## BELIZE
Consulate of Canada
85 Front Street
BELIZE CITY
Tel: (2) 33 722

## BOLIVIA
Australian Consulate
Edificio Montevideo Mezzanine
Av. Arce No. 2081
LA PAZ
Tel: (2) 244 0459

## BRAZIL
Australian Embassy
Shis QI 09
Conjuncto 16, Casa 01
CEP 70469-900
BRASILIA DF
Tel: (61) 248 5569

Australian Consulate
ANZ Group Representative Office
Avenida Nilo Pecanha 50, Grupo 810
RIO DE JANEIRO RJ 20044-900
Tel: (21) 240 2294

Australian Consulate-General
Rua Tenente Negrao 140
12 Andar Edificio,
Juscelino Kubitschek,Itiaim Bibi
SP 04530-030
SAO PAULO
Tel: (11) 3849 6281

■

## BULGARIA

Australian Consulate
37 Trakia Street
1504 SOFIA
Tel: (2) 946 1334

## BRUNEI

Australian High Commission
4th Floor, Teck Guan Plaza
Jalan Sultan
BANDAR SERI BEGAWAN BS8811
Tel: (2) 22 9435–6

## CAMBODIA

Australian Embassy
Villa 11, Street 254
R V Senei Vannavaut Oum
Daun Penh District
PHNOM PENH CITY
Tel: (23) 213 470

## CANADA

Australian High Commission
Suite 710, 50 O'Connor Street
OTTAWA, Ontario K1P 6L2
Tel: (613) 236 0841/783 7665

Australian Consulate-General
Suite 316, 175 Bloor Street, East
TORONTO, Ontario M4W 3R8
Tel: (416) 323 1155

Australian Consulate
World Trade Centre Complex
Suite 1225, 888 Dunsmuir Street
VANCOUVER, BC V6C 3K4
Tel: (604) 684 1177

## CHILE

Australian Embassy
Isidora Goyenechea 3621,
Las Condes
SANTIAGO DE CHILE
Tel: (2) 550 3500

## CHINA

Australian Embassy
21 Dongzhimenwai Dajie
Sanlitun
BEIJING 100600
Tel: (10) 6532 2331

Australian Consulate-General
1509 Main Building, GITIC Plaza
339 Huanshi Dong Lu
GUANGZHOU 510098
Tel: (20) 833 50909

Australian Consulate-General
Level 22, Citic Square
1168 Nanjing West Road
SHANGHAI 200041
Tel: (21) 5292 5500

## COLOMBIA

Australian Consulate
Carrera 18, No. 90-38,
BOGOTA
Tel: (1) 218 0942

## CÔTE D'IVOIRE

Canadian Embassy
Trade Centre, 23 Avenue Nogues
Le Plateau, ABIDJAN
Tel: 21 2009

## CROATIA

Australian Embassy
Kaptol Centar, 3rd Floor
Nova Ves II
10000 ZAGREB
Tel: (1) 489 1200

## CUBA

Canadian Embassy
Calle 30, No. 518 Esquina a7a
Miramar, HAVANA
Tel: (7) 24 2516

## CYPRUS

Australian High Commission
4 Annis Komninis Street
NICOSIA
Tel: (2) 27 53001–3

■

## CZECH REPUBLIC

Australian Consulate
6TH Floor
Solitaire Building
Klimentska ul.10
PRAGUE 110 001
Tel: (2) 5101 8350

## ECUADOR

Australian Consulate
Kennedy Norte, Calle San Roque y
Avda. Francisco de Orellana
Edificio Tecniseguros
GUAYAQUIL
Tel: (4) 680 823/800/700/655

## EGYPT

Australian Embassy
World Trade Centre, 11th Floor
Corniche El Nil
Boulac (Code 11111)
CAIRO
Tel: (2) 575 0444

## ESTONIA

Australian Consulate
Kopli 25
EE-104122 TALLINN
Tel: (6) 509 308

## ETHIOPIA

Canadian Embassy
Old Airport Area
Higher 23, Kebele 12, House 122
ADDIS ABABA
Tel: (1) 71 3022

## FIJI

Australian Embassy
37 Princes Road
Tamavua
SUVA
Tel: (3) 82211

## FINLAND

Australian Consulate
Museokatu 25B
FIN-00100 HELSINKI
Tel: (9) 44 7503

## FRANCE

Australian Embassy
4 Rue Jean Rey
75724 Cedex 15, PARIS
Tel: (01) 4059 3300/2

## FRENCH POLYNESIA

Australian Consulate
QANTAS Office, Vaima Centre
Papeete TAHITI
Tel: 43 8838

## GERMANY

Australian Embassy
Godesberger Allee 105–107
D-53175 BONN
Tel: (228) 81 030

Australian Embassy (Berlin Office)
Friedrichstrasse 200
BERLIN 10117
Tel: (30) 88 088-0

Australian Consulate-General
5th Floor, Gutleutstrasse 58-62
D-60322 FRANKFURT/M
Tel: (69) 90 558-0

## GHANA

Canadian High Commission
42 Independence Avenue, ACCRA
Tel: (21) 77 3791

## GREECE

Australian Embassy
37 Dimitriou Soutsou Street
Ambelokipi, ATHENS 11521
Tel: (1) 645 0404

Australian Consulate
20 Ionos Dragoumi Street
Thessaloniki 54624
Tel: (1) 240 706

## HAITI
Canadian Embassy
Bank of Nova Scotia
Delmas 18
PORT-AU-PRINCE
Tel: 23 2358

## HONG KONG
Australian Consulate-General
23rd Flr Harbour Centre
25 Harbour Road, Wanchai
HONG KONG
Tel: 2827 8881

## HUNGARY
Australian Embassy
Kiralyhago Ter 8–9
H-1126 BUDAPEST
Tel: (1) 457 9777

## ICELAND
Consulate-General of Canada
Suourlandsbraut 10
108 REYKJAVIK
Tel: (5) 68 0820

## INDIA
Australian High Commission
Australian Compound
No. 1/50 G Shantipath
Chanakyapuri
NEW DELHI 110-021
Tel: (11) 688 8223

Australian Consulate-General
16th Flr, Maker Towers E
Cuffe Parade, Colaba
MUMBAI 400-005
Tel: (22) 218 1071/2

## INDONESIA
Australian Embassy
Jalan H R Rasuna Said Kav C 15–16
JAKARTA SELATAN 12940
Tel: (21) 2550 5555

Australian Consulate
Jl. Prof Moh Yamin 4
Renon, DENPASAR
Tel: (361) 235092-3

## IRAN
Australian Embassy
No. 13, 23rd Street
Khalid Islambuli Avenue
TEHRAN 15138
Tel: (21) 872 4456

## IRELAND (EIRE)
Australian Embassy
Fitzwilton House
Wilton Terrace
DUBLIN 2
Tel: (1) 664 5300

## ISRAEL
Australian Embassy
Europe House, 4th Floor
37 Shaul Hamelech Boulevarde
TEL AVIV 64928
Tel: (3) 695 0451

## ITALY
Australian Embassy
Via Alessandria 215
ROME 00198
Tel: (6) 85 2721

Australian Consulate-General
3rd Floor, Via Borgogna 2
MILANO 20122
Tel: (2) 77 7041

## JAPAN

Australian Embassy
2-1-14 Mita
Minato-ku
TOKYO 108-8361
Tel: (3) 5232 4111

Australian Consulate-General
Twin 21 MID Tower, 26th Floor
2-1-61 Shiromi
Chuo-ku
OSAKA 540-6126
Tel: (6) 941 9448

## JORDAN

Australian Embassy
Between 4th & 5th Circles
Zahran Street
Jabel Amman
AMMAN
Tel: (6) 593 0246/7

## KAZAKHSTAN

Australian Embassy
20A Kazbek BI St
ALMATY 480100
Tel: (3272) 581 1600

## KENYA

Australian High Commission
Riverside Drive (off Chiromo Road)
NAIROBI
Tel: (2) 444 5034-9

## KIRIBATI

Australian High Commission
Bairiki
TARAWA
Tel: 21 184

## LAOS

Australian Embassy
Rue J Nehru
Quartier Phone Xay
VIENTIANE
Tel: (21) 41 3600

## LATVIA

Australian Consulate
Raina Bulvaris 3, RIGA LV-1050
Tel: 722 2385

## LEBANON

Australian Embassy
Farra Building, Rue Bliss
RAS BEIRUT
Tel: (1) 374 701

## LITHUANIA

Australian Consulate
Karmelitu 4/12
LI-2000 VILNIUS
Tel: (2) 22 3369/79 1448

## MADAGASCAR

Consulate of Canada
c/o QIT-Madagascar Minerals ltd
Lot II-M-62c, Villa Paule Androhibe
ANTANANARIVO 101
Tel: (2) 425 59

## MALAWI

Consulate of Canada
Accord Centre, Kamuzu Highway
BLANTYRE-LIMBE
Tel: 645 441

## MALAYSIA

Australian High Commission
6 Jalan Yap Kwan Seng
50450 KUALA LUMPUR
Tel: (3) 2146 5555

Australian Consulate
1C Lorong Hutton
10050 PENANG
Tel: (4) 263 3320

## MALTA

Australian High Commission
Ta'Xbiex Terrace
Ta'Xbiex MSD 11, MALTA
Tel: 33 8201

## MAURITIUS
Australian High Commission
2nd Floor, Rogers House
5 President John Kennedy Street
PORT LOUIS
Tel: 208 1700

## MEXICO
Australian Embassy
Ruben Dario 55
Col. Polanco
11580 MEXICO DF
Tel: (5) 531 5225

Australian Consulate
Av. Munich. No. 195 195 esq.
Nogala, col. Cuauhtemoc,
San Nicolas de los Garza
66450 MONTERREY
Tel: (81) 58 0791

## MICRONESIA
Australian Embassy
H & E Enterprises Building
Kolonia
POHNPEI
Tel: 320 5448

## MYANMAR
Australian Embassy
88 Strand Road
RANGOON
Tel: (1) 25 1809–10, 1797–98

## NEPAL
Australian Embassy
Bansbrai
KATHMANDU
Tel: (1) 371 678

## NETHERLANDS
Australian Embassy
Carnegielaan 4
2517 KH. THE HAGUE
Tel: (70) 310 8200

## NEW CALEDONIA
Australian Consulate-General
7th Floor, Immeuble Foch
19 Rue Du Maréchal Foch
NOUMEA
Tel: 27 2414

## NEW ZEALAND
Australian High Commission
72–78 Hobson Street
Thorndon
WELLINGTON
Tel: (4) 473 6411

Australian Consulate-General
7 PriceWaterHouseCoopers Tower
186,
194 Quay Street
AUCKLAND
Tel: (9) 303 2429/25

## NIGERIA
Australian High Commission
2 Ozumba Mbadiwe Avenue
Victoria Island
LAGOS
Tel: (1) 261 8875

## NORWAY
Australian Consulate
Jernbanetorget 2
OSLO
Tel: 224 79170

## PAKISTAN
Australian High Commission
Constituion Ave & Ispahani Road
Diplomatic Enclave No. 1
Sector G-5/4
ISLAMABAD
Tel: (51) 824345

Consulate of Canada
PAAF Building, 5th Floor
7D Kasmir–Egerton Road
LAHORE
Tel: (42) 636 6230

## PAPUA NEW GUINEA

Australian High Commission
Godwit Road
Waigani NCD
PORT MORESBY
Tel: 325 9333/9239

## PERU

Australian Consulate
Av. Victor Andrew
Belaunde 147,
Via Principal 155,
Torre Real Tres of. 1301
San Isidro
LIMA 27
Tel: (1) 222 8281

## PHILIPPINES

Australian Embassy
1st–5th Flrs, D. Salustiana Ty Tower
104 Paseo De Roxas, Makati
METRO MANILA
Tel: (2) 750 2850

## POLAND

Australian Embassy
ul. Nowogrodzka 11
WARSAW 00-513
Tel: (22) 5213 444

## ROMANIA

Australian Consulate
Blvd Unirii NS 74
Et 5, Sector 3
BUCHAREST 75103
Tel: (1) 320 9823

## RUSSIAN FEDERATION

Australian Embassy
13 Kropotkinsky Pereulok
MOSCOW 119034
Tel: (095) 956 6070

Consulate-General of Canada
32 Malodetskoselski Prospekt
ST PETERSBURG 198013
Tel: (812) 325 8448

Australian Consulate
42 Prospect Krasnogo Znameni
VLADIVOSTOK
Tel: (4232) 427 464

## SAUDI ARABIA

Australian Embassy
Diplomatic Quarter, RIYADH
Tel: (1) 488 7788

## SINGAPORE

Australian High Commission
25 Napier Road
SINGAPORE 258507
Tel: 65 6836 4100

## SLOVENIA

Australian Consulate
Trg Republike 3/XII
1000 LJUBLJANA
Tel: (61) 125 4252

## SOLOMON ISLANDS

Australian High Commission
Cnr Hibiscus Ave & Mud Alley
HONIARA
Tel: 21 561–3

## SOUTH AFRICA

Australian High Commission
14th Floor, BP Centre
Thibault Square
CAPE TOWN 8001
Tel: (21) 419 5425–9

Australian High Commission
292 Orient Street
Arcadia
PRETORIA 0083
Tel: (12) 342 3781

## SOUTH KOREA

Australian Embassy
11th Floor, Kyobo Building
1 Chongro-1-Ka
Chongro-Ku 110-714
SEOUL
Tel: (2) 730 6490

## SPAIN

Australian Embassy
Plaza del Descubridor
Diego de Ordas, 3
MADRID 28003
Tel: (1) 441 6025

Australian Consulate
9th Flr, Gran Via Carlos III No. 98
BARCELONA 08028
Tel: (3) 330 9496

## SRI LANKA

Australian High Commission
3 Cambridge Place
COLOMBO 7
Tel: (1) 69 8767

## SWEDEN

Australian Embassy
Sergels Torg 12
STOCKHOLM
Tel: (8) 613 2900

## SWITZERLAND

Australian Consulate-General
Chemins des Fins 2,
1211 GENEVA
Tel: (22) 799 9100

## SYRIA

Australian Embassy
128/A Farabi Street, East Villas
Mezzeh, DAMASCUS
Tel: (11) 613 2424

## TANZANIA

Canadian High Commission
38 Mirambo Street, Cnr Garden Ave
DAR-ES-SALAAM
Tel: (51) 46000–4

## THAILAND

Australian Embassy
37 South Sathorn Road
BANGKOK 10120
Tel: (2) 287 2680

Australian Consulate
165 Sirimungklajarn Road
Suthep, CHIANG MAI 50200
Tel: (53) 22 1083

## TONGA

Australian High Commission
Salote Road, NUKU'ALOFA
Tel: 23 244

## TUNISIA

Canadian Embassy
3 Rue de Senegal, Place d'Afrique
TUNIS
Tel: (1) 796 577

■

## TURKEY

Australian Embassy
83 Nenehatun Caddesi
Gaziosmanpasa
ANKARA
Tel: (312) 446 1180–7

Australian Consulate-General
Tepecik Yolu No. 58
Etiler, ISTANBUL
Tel: (212) 257 7050

## UKRAINE

Australian Consulate
18 Kominterna Ul, Apt 11, KYIV
Tel: (044) 235 4481

## UNITED ARAB EMIRATES

Australian Consulate-General
6th Flr, Dubai World Trade Centre
DUBAI
Tel: (4) 31 3444

## UNITED KINGDOM

Australian High Commission
Australia House
The Strand
LONDON WC2B 4LA
Tel: (171) 379 4334

Australian Consulate
1st Floor, Century House,
11 St Peter's Square
MANCHESTER M2 3DN
Tel: (161) 273 9440

## UNITED STATES OF AMERICA

Australian Embassy
1601 Massachusetts Avenue, NW
WASHINGTON DC 20036-2273
Tel: (202) 797 3000

Australian Consulate-General
Onee Buckhead Plaza
3060 Peachtree Road, NW
ATLANTA GA 30305
Tel: (404) 760 3400

Australian Consulate
20 Park Plaza, Suite 457
BOSTON MA 02116
Tel: (617) 542 8655

Australian Consulate-General
Penthouse, 1000 Bishop Street
HONOLULU HI 96813
Tel: (808) 524 5050

Australian Consulate-General
Century Plaza Towers, 19th Flr
2049 Century Park East
LOS ANGELES CA 90067
Tel: (310) 229 4800

Australian Consulate-General
34th Flr, 150 East 42nd Street
NEW YORK NY 10017-5612
Tel: (212) 351 6500

Australian Consulate-General
Suite 200, 625 Market Street
SAN FRANCISCO CA 94105-3304
Tel: (415) 536 1970

## URUGUAY

Australian Consulate
Cerro Largo 1000
MONTEVIDEO
Tel: (2) 901 0743

## VANUATU

Australian High Commission
KPMG House
PORT VILA
Tel: 22 777

## VENEZUELA

Australian Embassy
Av. Francisco de Miranda,
cruce con ave. Sur Piso Uno,
Altamira CARACAS 1060
Tel: (2) 263 4033

## VIETNAM

Australian Embassy
8 Dao Tan Street
Ba Dinh, HANOI
Tel: (4) 831 7711

## WESTERN SAMOA

Australian High Commission
2nd Floor, NPF Building
Beach Road
APIA
Tel: 23 411

## YEMEN

Consulate of Canada
Yemen Computer Co. Ltd
Bldg 4, 11th Street, off Haddah St
SANAA
Tel: (1) 208 814

## YUGOSLAVIA

Australian Embassy
13 Cika Ljubina
11000 BELGRADE
Tel: (11) 62 4655

## ZIMBABWE

Australian High Commission
29 Mazowe Street
The Avenues, HARARE
Tel: (4) 25 3661

■

# ■ N E W   Z E A L A N D ■
## ■ E M B A S S I E S ■

**ARGENTINA**
New Zealand Consulate
Carlos Pelligrini 1427
Piso 51011, BUENOS AIRES
Tel: (1) 328 0747

**AUSTRALIA**
New Zealand High Commission
Commonwealth Ave
CANBERRA ACT 2600
Tel: (2) 6270 4211

**AUSTRIA**
New Zealand Consulate-General
Springsiedelgasse 28,
A-1190 VIENNA
Tel: (1) 318 8505

**BELGIUM**
New Zealand Embassy
Boulevard de Regent 47–48
1000 BRUSSELS
Tel: (2) 512 1040

**BRAZIL**
New Zealand Consulate-General
Rua Hungria
88860, CEP 01455
SAO PAULO
Tel: (11) 212 2288

**BRUNEI**
New Zealand Consulate
35A Seri Lambak Shopping Centre
Jalan, Berakas
BANDAR SERI BEGAWAN 1927
Tel: (2) 331 010

**CANADA**
New Zealand High Commission
Suite 727, Metropolitan House
99 Bank St
OTTAWA K1P 6G3
Tel: (613) 238 5991

New Zealand Consulate-General
Suite 1200–888, Dunsmuir St
VANCOUVER, BC V6C 3K4
Tel: (604) 684 7388

**CHILE**
New Zealand Embassy
Avenida Isidora Goyenechea 3516
Casilla 112, Correo
Las Condes
SANTIAGO DE CHILE
Tel: (2) 231 4204

**CHINA**
New Zealand Embassy
Ritan Dongerjie No. 1
Chao Yang District, BEIJING
Tel: (10) 6532 2731/2/3/4

New Zealand Consulate-General
Qi Hua Tower
15A 1375 Huai Hai Rd (c)
SHANGHAI 200031
Tel: (21) 6431 0226

**COLOMBIA**
New Zealand Consulate
Diagonal 109, 1–39 Este
Apt 401, Santa Ana
(A.A. 30402) BOGOTA
Tel: (1) 32 100 0836

146
■

## COOK ISLANDS

New Zealand High Commission
Philatelic Bureau Building
Takuvaine Rd, Avarua
RAROTONGA
Tel: 22 201

## CYPRUS

New Zealand Consulate
Action Public Relations and Publicity Ltd
36 Ayion Nicolaou St
NICOSIA
Tel: (2) 590 555

## CZECH REPUBLIC

New Zealand Consulate
Dykova 19
101 00 PRAGUE 10
Tel: (2) 254 198

## FIJI

New Zealand Embassy
Reserve Bank of Fiji Building
Pratt St, PO Box 1378
SUVA
Tel: 311 422

## FINLAND

New Zealand Consulate
Matkatoimisto Finlandia
Kruunuvuorenkatu 5A
00160 HELSINKI
Tel: (9) 065 9100

## FRANCE

New Zealand Embassy
7 ter, rue Leonard de Vinci
75116 PARIS
Tel: (01) 4500 2411

## FRENCH POLYNESIA

New Zealand Consulate
c/o Air New Zealand Ltd
Vaima Centre (BP 73)
Papeete, TAHITI
Tel: 430 170

## GERMANY

New Zealand Embassy
Bundeskanzlerplatz 2–10
53113 BONN
Tel: (228) 228 070
New Zealand Consulate-General
Heimhuderstrasse 56
20148 HAMBURG
Tel: (40) 442 5550

## GREECE

New Zealand Consulate-General
c/o Coopers and Lybrand
24 Xenias St
ATHENS 11528
Tel: (1) 771 0112

## GUAM

New Zealand Consulate
290 Salas St
Tamuning
GUAM 96931
Tel: (671) 646 1061

## HONG KONG

New Zealand Consulate-General
3416 Jardine House, Connaught Rd
HONG KONG
Tel: 2525 5044

## HUNGARY

New Zealand Consulate
Teréz krt, 38
1066 BUDAPEST
Tel: (1) 131 4908

## INDIA

New Zealand High Commission
50N Nyaya Marg
Chanakyapuri
NEW DELHI 110-021
Tel: (11) 688 3170

■

## INDONESIA
New Zealand Embassy
BR1 11 Building
23rd flr
Jl. Jend. Sudirman Kav
44–46,
JAKARTA
Tel: (62 21) 570 9560

## IRAN
New Zealand Embassy
57 Jarad Sarafraz (Darya e Noor)
Ostad Motahari Ave
TEHRAN 11365
Tel: (21) 875 7052

## IRELAND (EIRE)
New Zealand Consulate-General
46 Upper Mount St
DUBLIN 2
Tel: (1) 676 2464

## ITALY
New Zealand Embassy
Via Zara 28
ROME 00198
Tel: (6) 440 2928

New Zealand Consulate-General
Via Guido d'Arezzo 6
MILAN 20145
Tel: (2) 4801 2544

## JAPAN
New Zealand Embassy
20–40 Kamiyama-cho
Shibuya-ku
TOKYO 150
Tel: (3) 3467 2271/5

New Zealand Consulate-General
MID Tower, Twin 21
2-1-61 Shironmi
Chuo-ku
OSAKA 540
Tel: (6) 942 9016

## JORDAN
New Zealand Consulate
Khalaf Building
99 King Hussein St
PO Box 586
AMMAN
Tel: (6) 636 720 / 625 149

## KENYA
New Zealand Consulate
Minet ICDC Insurance
Minet House, Nyerere Rd,
NAIROBI
Tel: (2) 722 467

## KIRIBATI
New Zealand High Commission
PO Box 53
TARAWA
Tel: 21 400

## MALAYSIA
New Zealand High Commission
Menara IMC
8 Jalan Sultan Ismail
PO Box 12-003
50764 KUALA LUMPUR
Tel: (3) 2078 2533

New Zealand Consulate
Lot 8679, Section 64
Pending Commercial Centre
93762 Kuching
SARAWAK
Tel: 331 411

## MALTA
New Zealand Consulate
Villa Hampstead
Oliver Agius St
BZN03 ATTARD
Tel: 43 5025

■

## MAURITIUS
New Zealand Consulate
Anchor Building
Les Pailles, BELL VILLAGE
Tel: 212 4920

## MEXICO
New Zealand Embassy
Jose Luis Lagrange 103
Colonia Los Morales
Polanco
11510 MEXICO
Tel: (5) 281 5486

## NEPAL
New Zealand Consulate
Dilli Bazar
KATHMANDU
Tel: (1) 412 436

## NETHERLANDS
New Zealand Embassy
Carnegielaan 4
2517 KH. THE HAGUE
Tel: (70) 346 9324

## NIUE
New Zealand High Commission
Tapeu, Alofi
PO Box 78 NIUE
Tel: 4022

## NORWAY
New Zealand Consulate-General
Løvenskidd-Vaekerø AS
Drammensun 230
0212 OSLO 2
Tel: (47) 6684 9530

## OMAN
New Zealand Consulate
PO Box 520 Muscat
SULTANATE OF OMAN
Tel: 794 932 / 795 726

## PAKISTAN
New Zealand  Consulate-General
74/1A Lalazar
Moulvi Tamizuddin Khan Rd
KARACHI
Tel: (21) 561 0198 / 561 0960

## PAPUA NEW GUINEA
New Zealand High Commission
Waigani PO Box 1051
PORT MORESBY
Tel: 325 9444

## PERU
New Zealand Consulate
Camino Real 390
Piso 17, Torre Central
San Isidro
LIMA
Tel: (1) 442 9317

## PHILIPPINES
New Zealand Embassy
23rd Floor, Far East Bank Centre
Sen Gil Puyat Ave
1272 Makati City, MANILA
Tel: (2) 891 5358

## POLAND
New Zealand Consulate
Natpoll Business Centre
Ul Migdolowa 4
02-760 WARSAW
Tel: (22) 645 1407

## PORTUGAL
New Zealand Consulate
Rua de S. Felix,
13–2
1200 LISBOA
Tel: (1) 350 9690

## RUSSIAN FEDERATION
New Zealand Embassy
44 Ulitsa Povarskaya
MOSCOW 121069
Tel: (095) 956 3579

■

## SAUDI ARABIA

New Zealand Embassy
Diplomatic Quarter
PO Box 94397
RIYADH 11693
Tel: (1) 488 7988

## SINGAPORE

New Zealand High Commission
391A Orchard Rd
15-06/10 Ngee Ann City
Tower A, SINGAPORE
Tel: 235 9966

## SOLOMON ISLANDS

New Zealand High Commission
City Centre Building
Mendana Ave
HONIARA
Tel: 21 502 / 503

## SOUTH AFRICA

New Zealand High Commission
Block C, Hatfield Gardens
1110 Arcadia St
PRETORIA 0028
Tel: (12) 342 8656

New Zealand Consulate
Birthday Hill
4 Kirstenbosch Drive
Bishopscourt
CAPE TOWN 7700
Tel: (21) 619 978

## SOUTH KOREA

New Zealand Embassy
Rooms 1802–1805, Kyobo Building
1 Chongro 1-KA
Chongro-Ku
GPO Box 1059
SEOUL
Tel: (2) 730 7794 / 95

## SPAIN

New Zealand Embassy
Plaza de La Lealtad 2
28014 MADRID
Tel: (1) 523 0226

New Zealand Consulate
Travesera de Gracia 64
08006 BARCELONA
Tel: (93) 209 0399

## SRI LANKA

New Zealand Consulate
c/o Aitken Spence & Co. Ltd
PO Box 5 COLOMBO
Tel: (1) 32 7861 / 869

## SWEDEN

New Zealand Consulate-General
Nybrogatan 34
S-11439
STOCKHOLM
Tel: (8) 611 2625

## SWITZERLAND

New Zealand Consulate-General
28A Chemin de Petit-Saconnex
CH-1209 GENEVA
Tel: (22) 734 9530

## THAILAND

New Zealand Embassy
M Thai Tower
14th Floor
All Seasons Plca
87 Wireless Rd
BANGKOK 10330
Tel: (2) 254 2530

## TONGA

New Zealand High Commission
Cnr Taufa'ahau & Salote Roads
NUKU'ALOFA
Tel: 23 122

## TURKEY

New Zealand Embassy
Iran Caddesi 13
Kavaklidere 06700
ANKARA
Tel: (312) 467 9054 /6 /8

New Zealand Consulate
Maya akar Center 100/102
Buyukdere Cadessi
Estentepe 80280
ISTANBUL
Tel: (212) 275 2989

## UNITED KINGDOM

New Zealand High Commission
New Zealand House
The Haymarket
LONDON SW1Y 4TQ
Tel: (171) 930 8422

New Zealand Consulate
The Ballance House
118A Lisburn Rd, Glenavy
Co. Antrim, BT 29 4NY
NORTHERN IRELAND
Tel: (1846) 648 098

## UNITED STATES OF AMERICA

New Zealand Embassy
37 Observatory Circle NW
WASHINGTON DC 20008
Tel: (202) 328 4800

New Zealand Consulate
513 Seminole Ave NE
ATLANTA GA 30307
Tel: (404) 525 2495

New Zealand Consulate
8600 Bryn Mawr Ave
Suite 500N
CHICAGO IL 60631
Tel: (773) 714 9461

New Zealand Consulate-General
Suite 1150
12400 Wilshire Boulevard
LOS ANGELES CA 90025
Tel: (310) 207 1605

New Zealand Consulate-General
780 Third Avenue
NEW YORK NY 10017-2024
Tel: (212) 832 4038

New Zealand Consulate-General
One Maritime Plaza
Suite 700
SAN FRANCISCO CA 94111
Tel: (415) 399 1255

## URUGUAY

New Zealand Consulate
Boulevar Artigas 1074
MONTEVIDEO
Tel: (2) 785 925 / 786 143

## VANUATU

New Zealand High Commission
BDO House
Kumul Highway
PORT VILA
Tel: 22 933

## VENEZUELA

New Zealand Consulate
c/o New Zealand Milk Products
Venezuela SA
Torre La Noria
Piso 10, Ofcina 10-B4
Pases Henrique Eraso
San Roman, CARACAS
Tel: (2) 924 332

**VIETNAM**

New Zealand Embassy
32 Hang Bai St
HANOI
Tel: (4) 241 480

New Zealand Consulate-General
41 Nguyen Thi Minh Khai St
District 1
HO CHI MINH CITY
Tel: (8) 211 933

**WESTERN SAMOA**

New Zealand High Commission
Beach Road
APIA
Tel: 21 711

**ZIMBABWE**

New Zealand High Commission
Eastgate Centre
Cnr Robert Mugabe Rd & Second St
HARARE
Tel: (4) 75 9221

# ■ TRAVEL - RELATED ■
## ■ WEBSITES ■

| Website | Address |
|---|---|

**AltaVista Translation Service**     **http://babel.altavista.com/**
*Provides English translations from French, Spanish, Italian, German and Portuguese, and vice versa.*

---

**Berkeley's Foreign**     **www.itp.berkeley.edu/~thorne/HumanResources.html**
**Language Resources**
*University of Berkeley's guide to the world's language and culture resources.*

---

**Centers for Disease Control and Prevention**     **www.cdc.gov/travel**
*Lists of and information on countries infected by cholera, yellow fever and plague, with disease reports for each continent.*

---

**Cyber Adventures**     **www.cyber-adventures.com**
*Travelogues, essays, 'strange but true' travel stories, reports on all destinations, with 'tips and tricks'.*

---

**Department of Foreign Affairs & Trade**     **www.dfat.gov.au**
*Useful section containing travel warnings and consular advice, together with information on world 'hot spots' and embassy/consulate contact details.*

---

**Excite Travel**     **www.city.net**
*Reservations, info for frequent flyers, details on cultural and sporting events, cheapest US fares and local weather in major cities around the world.*

---

**Fielding's Travel Guides**     **www.fieldingtravel.com**
*International list of volunteer organisations and possible casual work.*

---

**Foreign Languages For Travellers**     **www.travlang.com/languages**
*Direct translation from (or to) almost any language.*

---

**IAMAT**     **www.iamat.org**
*Information on IAMAT (International Association for Medical Treatment to Travellers), but no directory for member clinics.*

---

| Website | Address |
|---|---|

**International Language Development** — www.ild.com
*Lessons in French, German, Japanese, Korean, Russian and Spanish.*

**Internet Cafes** — www.netcafeguide.com
*Complete guide to Internet Cafes around the globe.*

**Internet Guide To Hostelling** — www.hostels.com
*Although not officially linked with the Youth Hostel Association, provides an exhaustive list of hostels and budget accommodation for all destinations.*

**Internet Travel Network** — www.itn.com
*US-based reservations system, information on any region and all aspects of travel.*

**Lonely Planet Online** — www.lonelyplanet.com
*In-depth information on all apects of travelling. Easy-to-navigate site for links to other travel-related websites, travellers' e-mail free-for-all, as well as details on all Lonely Planet publications.*

**MapQuest** — www.mapquest.com
*Provides regional, national and city maps for the world.*

**Micronations** — http://members.tripod.com/rittergeist/
*List of ephemeral states, model nations, imaginary states, counter-countries and unrecognised nations.*

**Mysterious Places** — mysteriousplaces.com
*Historical and cultural background on sacred locations and places of geological interest worldwide.*

**One-World Global Calendar** — www.zapcom.net/phoenix.arabeth/1world.html
*Lists holidays, festivals and other important dates throughout the world.*

**Rough Guides Online** — www.roughguides.com
*Details on most countries, US air flights, travellers' newsletter, and information on all Rough Guides travel and music publications.*

**Shoreland's Travel Health Online** — www.tripprep.com
*General health tips and country health profiles with suggested precautions and advice from the US Department of State.*

| Website | Address |
|---|---|
| **Tourism Offices Worldwide Directory** | **www.towd.com** |
| *Directory of tourist authorities and diplomatic offices around the world.* | |
| **Travel Basics** | **www.ciee.org/zone/planner/basics.htm** |
| *Basic travel tips and advice, such as useful packing checklist. US site, but relevant to all budget-travellers/students.* | |
| **Travel-Library** | **www.travel-library.com** |
| *Extensive list of travelogues, journals and photos, by subject and country.* | |
| **Traveller's Medical & Vaccination Centre** | **www.tmvc.com.au** |
| *Country-by-country vaccination requirements, with a reference section on health reports and studies on infectious diseases.* | |
| **Travelocity** | **www.travelocity.com** |
| *Flight reservations, car rentals, hotel bookings (mostly within the US), also has travel essays.* | |
| **Universal Currency Converter** | **www.xe.net/currency** |
| *Allows instant conversion for all the world's currencies.* | |
| **Web Of Culture** | **www.worldculture.com/index.html** |
| *Information on local etiquette, customs and national cultures.* | |
| **World Health Organization** | **www.who.ch** |
| *Information on WHO generally, details on WHO vacancies and a register for disease outbreaks around the world.* | |
| **World Travel Guide** | **www.wtgonline.com** |
| *Quality site for information on most countries of the world.* | |
| **Worldwide Brochures** | **www.wwb.com** |
| *Access to information on maps, guides, brochures, etc., for any destination, together with relevant government office or travel company.* | |

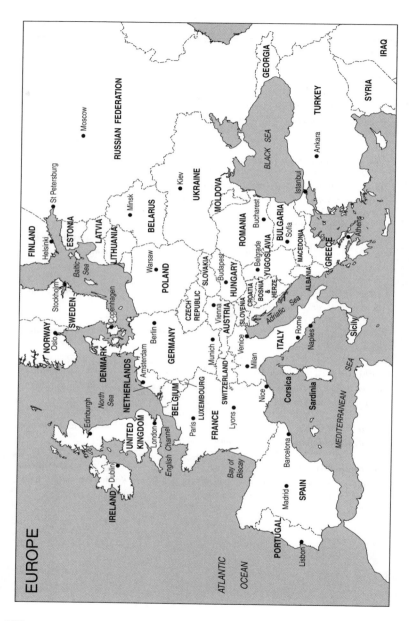

EUROPE

ATLANTIC OCEAN

IRELAND
Dublin
UNITED KINGDOM
Edinburgh
London
English Channel
North Sea

NORWAY
Oslo
Stockholm
SWEDEN
Baltic Sea
FINLAND
Helsinki
St Petersburg
ESTONIA
LATVIA
LITHUANIA

DENMARK
Copenhagen
NETHERLANDS
Amsterdam
BELGIUM
LUXEMBOURG
Berlin
GERMANY
Munich

RUSSIAN FEDERATION
Moscow

BELARUS
Minsk
Warsaw
POLAND

UKRAINE
Kiev

MOLDOVA

ROMANIA
Bucharest

GEORGIA

CZECH REPUBLIC
SLOVAKIA
Vienna
AUSTRIA
Budapest
HUNGARY
SLOVENIA
CROATIA
BOSNIA & HERZE
YUGOSLAVIA
Belgrade

BULGARIA
Sofia
MACEDONIA
ALBANIA
GREECE
Athens
Istanbul
BLACK SEA
TURKEY
Ankara
SYRIA
IRAQ

SWITZERLAND
Venice
Milan
Nice
Adriatic Sea

FRANCE
Paris
Lyons
Bay of Biscay

ITALY
Rome
Naples
Corsica
Sardinia
Sicily

MEDITERRANEAN SEA

SPAIN
Madrid
Barcelona
PORTUGAL
Lisbon

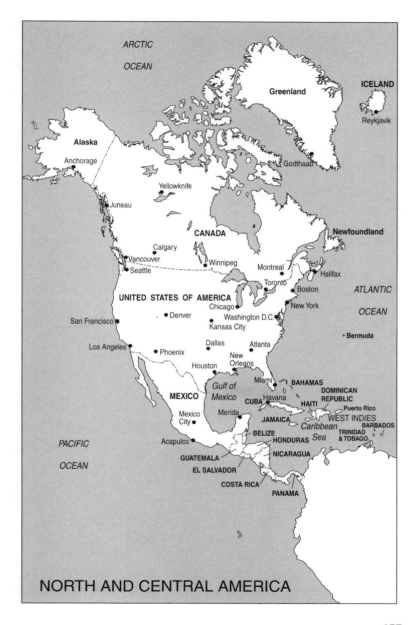

NORTH AND CENTRAL AMERICA

SOUTH AMERICA

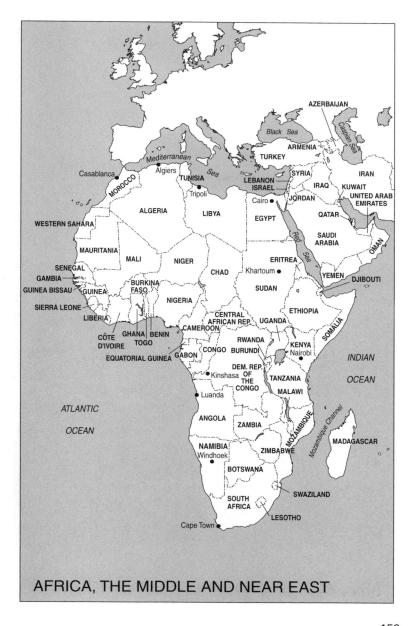

AFRICA, THE MIDDLE AND NEAR EAST

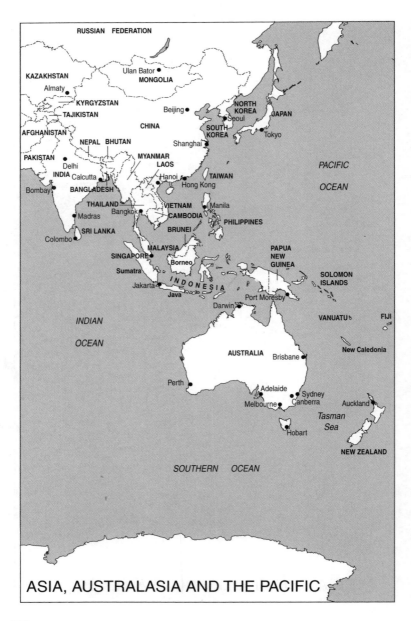

ASIA, AUSTRALASIA AND THE PACIFIC